# THE
# TOP **10** DISTINCTIONS
## BETWEEN

# Winners

—— AND ——

# Whiners

# Other books by Keith Cameron Smith

# THE
# TOP **10** DISTINCTIONS
## BETWEEN

# Winners

=== AND ===

# Whiners

## KEITH CAMERON SMITH

**WILEY**

John Wiley & Sons, Inc.

Published by John Wiley & Sons, Inc., Hoboken, New Jersey.
Published simultaneously in Canada.

For general information on our other products and services or for technical support, please contact our Customer Care Department within the United States at (800) 762-2974, outside the United States at (317) 572-3993 or fax (317) 572-4002.

Wiley also publishes its books in a variety of electronic formats. Some content that appears in print may not be available in electronic books. For more information about Wiley products, visit our web site at www.wiley.com.

ISBN 978-0-470-88586-4 (cloth); ISBN 978-0-470-91848-7 (ebk);
ISBN 978-0-470-91849-4 (ebk); ISBN 978-0-470-91850-0 (ebk)

Printed in the United States of America.

10  9  8  7  6  5  4  3  2  1

# Contents

*Contents*

# *Preface*

Winners have certain beliefs and behaviors that empower them to win. We have developed perspectives that create consistent results in our lives that are positive. Whiners, on the other hand, have learned bad habits in their thoughts, words, and actions that cause pain and problems. By learning the positive beliefs and behaviors of winners and unlearning the negative beliefs and behaviors of whiners, you can take control of your life and win more consistently.

The primary reason I wrote this book was simply to help people win more consistently in each area of their lives. I chose to use the word *whiner* instead of *loser* in the title of this book because whining is one of the biggest enemies of winning. In my opinion, it is very often whining that leads to losing. I have seen many people suffer for years because of their continual whining. Whining, or complaining, is destructive. Many people have destroyed relationships, businesses, and even their dreams because of whining.

The distinctions I write about winners in this book are the ones that have allowed me to develop and enjoy good relationships, to be successful in business, and to make measurable progress toward my dreams. I will be the first one to tell you that I have not mastered all of the beliefs and behaviors of winners in these distinctions but I practice them every day. I am pretty good at some of them, but I still have a lot of practicing to do before I consistently reap the benefits of some others. Wherever you find yourself in life right now, these distinctions can help you improve the quality of your life. Whether you are a chronic whiner who is continually causing yourself problems or if you already consider yourself a winner, I ask you to take two or three of these distinctions and put them into practice immediately and see if they don't produce some positive results in your life. By choosing to change some of your beliefs and behaviors, you can and will win more consistently in each area of life. Just the fact that you are reading this book tells me you already are a winner. The truth is we all whine sometimes, but as we learn to whine less we will win more!

I also want to mention three other reasons why I wrote this book. They are the same reasons I wrote *The Top 10 Distinctions between Millionaires and the Middle Class* and am now developing this series. They are responsibility, purpose, and legacy. As I wrote in the preface to the millionaire book, I believe we all have a responsibility to share those things that produce positive results in our own lives. Also, I experience a strong sense of purpose each time I teach these distinctions in various venues around the world. And I see these books as part of my legacy, especially to my own children. Some of my favorite books are over 100 years old. It's fascinating to think that someone may be reading, enjoying, and benefiting from this book 100 years from now. I strongly believe that these distinctions between winners and whiners are timeless. They are just as relevant today as they were 100 years ago and they will be just as relevant 100 years from now. Read, enjoy, and benefit from these distinctions. You already are a winner!

# *A Note on the Order of the Distinctions*

I have arranged the distinctions in descending order of importance. This arrangement is based on my own experiences as well as the lessons I have learned from people who I consider to be true winners in life. The importance of these distinctions could be rearranged to fit your own life during the season you are going through. For instance, Distinction 7 may be more important to you than Distinction 3 at this time in your life. So whichever distinction resonates with you the strongest and speaks to your heart the loudest, listen to it and learn what life is trying to teach you. As you work with these distinctions, I think you will find that Distinction 1 is the most important to work with throughout your life. Always remember, being a winner is not a onetime event, it is a lifelong journey.

# THE TOP **10** DISTINCTIONS
## BETWEEN

# Winners

=== AND ===

# Whiners

# Distinction 10

Winners take responsibility.
Whiners play the victim.

L et's face it: Life doesn't always go according to plan. In fact, it's been said that life is what happens while you're making other plans.

To become a winner in the face of this unpredictability requires that you balance two seemingly contradictory ideas. The first is best expressed by the expression "If it's going to be, it's up to me." The second is nearly the opposite: "What will be, will be."

These two statements sound fine by themselves—but when you put them side-by-side they contradict each other. And yet, taking either of these statements to the extreme produces negative results.

For example, let's look at the first statement: *If it's going to be, it's up to me*. Taking that philosophy to an extreme leads to arrogance and the perception that you don't need anyone. And the second statement? Taken to its extreme, the idea that *what will be, will be* leads to the role of victim, a person aimlessly drifting with no sense of control.

The truth lies somewhere in the middle. Winners seek to find a balance in life, and the balance point for these two statements is responsibility. Responsibility means that you do your best and trust that good will result. You can't always live in a state of *what will be, will be*, or you'll never take positive action. You can't always live in a state of *if it's going to be, it's up to me*, or you will think more highly of yourself than you should and become arrogant and judgmental.

These extremes—a lack of perceived control and a state of arrogance—start whiners down a dangerous path that leads to only one place: fear. That sense of fear manifests itself in people as worry, and worry is the enemy of winning.

Winners don't worry; whiners do.

Conversely, while fear is faith that the worst will happen, winners have faith in positive outcomes, and that faith manifests itself in the form of trust—a belief in the good in people and situations. While there may be people who do not have good intentions toward you, most probably do. Winners look for those who do—and don't worry about the rest.

Winners trust the intentions of others. Whiners play the victim because they allow their fears to grow into worry, their worry to grow into suspicion, and their suspicion to grow into division. You can't be a winner without others. Life is a team sport. Whining leads to separation, but winning comes only through unity.

The decision to live by faith or fear is just that: a decision. It is a personal choice and it is one you must make every day. Your choices are your responsibility. A whiner thinks his choices depend on his circumstances and that those circumstances are someone else's fault.

Fear is rooted in a belief that you have no choice. In reality, your circumstances exist because of your choices, and those choices are made in the context of either faith or fear. Accept the responsibility to make choices based on faith and you become a winner. Make choices based on fear and you will be a whiner.

Winners know we always have choices, and they take responsibility for them. Whiners, however, believe that their choices are controlled by someone else. And while you can let someone else control your choices, isn't that a choice in itself? Becoming a winner is impossible until you assume the responsibility of choice. Winners understand that power, and use it wisely.

Whiners play the victim by blaming others for their circumstances. Whiners say, "If only they had done this, or if only they hadn't done that, my life would be perfect." Blaming and complaining go hand-in-hand, and victims do a lot of both. Remember: Choices determine circumstances; circumstances do not determine choices. As long as you whine about your circumstances, you cannot become a winner.

Is there something in your life that you've been blaming others for that has been holding you back? As long as you are blaming and complaining, you remain the same. Taking responsibility for your circumstances is the first step toward growth.

There have been many situations in my life that I blamed others for. But I have learned that as long as I play the victim by blaming and complaining, I battle with feelings of disappointment and discouragement. Once, when I related a disappointment to my friend Nido Qubein, he told me, "Keith, it is okay to be disappointed. It's not okay to be discouraged."

The truth is that we all face disappointment. When we become disappointed, though, we must learn to encourage ourselves before we become discouraged, for following discouragement is depression.

Whiners battle with depression. Winners deal with their disappointments, encourage themselves, and move on. A winner says, "My thoughts, feelings, and actions are my responsibility." Winning starts with your thoughts, and taking responsibility for them means choosing positive ones.

Whining is the fruit of negative thinking. Don't let others fill your mind with negative thoughts. Make conscious choices on what you hold in your mind, for what you allow to stay there makes you either a winner or a whiner.

Winners choose to be winners. Winners take responsibility for the thoughts, feelings, and actions that produce their circumstances. Whiners let others control their thoughts, and then blame them for the results.

Results are reflections—simple reflections of the choices you make. Winners see almost everything in their lives as a result, or a reflection. Health is, most of the time, a result or reflection of the choices you make about eating and exercising. Wealth is a result or reflection of the choices you make about money. Happiness is a result or reflection of the thoughts you think. You must learn to take responsibility for the choices you make in each area of life. If you don't, then you will feel like a victim and the results you get will be negative. Instead of health, there will be sickness. Instead of wealth, there will be poverty. Instead of happiness, there will be depression. Positive and negative results are simply reflections of the choices we make, especially the choices we make concerning our thoughts.

Now let's look at your results as fruits on a tree. Just as whining is the fruit of negative thinking, winning is the fruit of positive thinking. The positive results you desire are the fruits of positive thoughts, which are the roots of the plant. Winners understand that our roots create our fruits. Say to yourself: My roots create my fruits. Winners take responsibility for their results by taking responsibility for their thoughts.

Winners see thoughts like seeds and their minds like fertile soil. The thoughts you choose to hold in your mind will start growing roots and eventually a little thought or seed can become a big tree with lots of fruit. So be careful to hold positive thoughts in your mind.

When negative thoughts appear, which they most certainly will, don't let them stay for very long or they will start to grow roots. Once a thought has started to grow roots, it becomes harder to remove. Winners believe "my results are my responsibility." That's why we choose our thoughts carefully. We choose to think about what we do want, not what we don't want. Whiners waste their time thinking about the things they don't want; and that's what they get in their lives. Whiners become victims because they allow others to control their thoughts. We all want to win more consistently in our lives. To be a winner you must consistently control your thoughts. By controlling your thoughts, you can change your results. Winners take responsibility for their results by controlling their thoughts.

**Winners take responsibility.**
**Whiners play the victim.**

# Distinction 9

Winners can have what they want.
Whiners want what they cannot have.

What do you want? Are you willing to pay the price to get it? Everything has a price, and while whiners want something for nothing, winners work hard in pursuit of their passions.

Sometimes hard work is part of the price we pay to get what we want. At other times, things come to us easily and without much effort, and the price we pay is humility, which is to "let go and let God." There have been times in my life when I have taken my hands off the metaphorical wheel and said, "This is beyond me right now. I don't know how to make this happen yet." Lo and behold, it seems to happen automatically.

*Distinction 9*

Winners know when to press on and when to let go. Whiners press on—until the first obstacle—but instead of trusting that the right outcome will happen, they let go. Winners let go and trust. Whiners let go and fear.

Whiners believe that other people should provide for them. They feel that because others have more, they are entitled to some of it. This entitlement mentality is extremely destructive and leads whiners to a state of self-pity, where they live in a constant quest for sympathy and focus all their energy on how hard life is and why they can't do this or that.

Winners, on the other hand, look at people who have more than they do and believe: "If others can do it, so can I." Then they learn what they need to do to get it.

Most wealthy people weren't handed their wealth—they earned it. Winners understand that they can learn to acquire what they desire. You can learn to earn whatever amount of money you desire. You can learn how to be healthy. You can learn how to have deep and meaningful relationships. You can learn to acquire whatever it is you desire.

Part of the price is knowledge. Do you invest in expanding your mind? Are you learning new things?

Limitations are simply due to a lack of knowledge. If you see someone winning in an area where you're losing, it's simply because they know something that you don't know and they are choosing to apply it. You can learn whatever it is you need to know to get whatever it is that you want.

Another price that winners pay to get what they want is criticism. It's windy at the top of the ladder, and criticism can be the price of success. Ironically, whiners are the critics. Because they believe the lie that they can't have something, they criticize those who do have it—whether "it" is wealth, rich relationships, health, or joy.

Whiners are critical because they aren't willing to pay the price of success themselves. Winners pay the price, even when that price is high, and accept that criticism is a part of life. Winners don't worry about what others think of them. They care what they think of themselves.

How do you feel about yourself? Do you nourish your self-respect? Do you like. . . . you? Winners have high self-esteem. But, while they think well of themselves, they are not conceited or arrogant; they simply believe in their abilities. Whiners think poorly

**15**

of themselves, and criticize others because they have a habit of criticizing themselves.

Winners don't listen to the critics; they listen to their hearts. They are not consumed by what others think about them.

A powerful insight to remember is the 20-40-60 principle, which is: "When you're 20 years old, you care what everyone thinks about you. When you're 40 years old, you don't care what anyone thinks about you. When you're 60 years old, you finally realize that nobody was thinking about you at all."

People are consumed by their own lives—they aren't thinking about you all the time. Even when someone criticizes you, he isn't thinking about you five minutes later. If you've been worrying about what others think, I have three words for you: Get over it.

Whiners live in a constant state of negative energy, critical of almost everything, and consumed by their own egos and the opinions of others. Winners know that it's not all about them, and they willingly pay another winner's price—service.

Zig Ziglar once said, "If you help enough other people get what they want, you can have anything you want." Winners have an innate grasp of service and understand that when they serve others from the heart, it's a sign that they are doing things for the right reasons. Serving people from the head just so you can get what you want may work to a certain degree, but it removes the joy of service—and the joy that comes from serving from the heart is worth more than anything you could possibly desire. Service that flows from the heart is a price that's a joy and a privilege to pay.

Whiners can't have what they want because of ignorance, low self-esteem, and lack of service. Increase your knowledge about what you do want, ignore criticism, and serve people from your heart—and you can have what you want.

So what do you want and why do you want it? The why question is very important because the things you think you want could just be the things someone else wanted for you. This is also important because if you don't understand why you want something then you will not be willing to pay the prices to get it. Winners are successful and fulfilled because they not only know what they want, they are also clear on why they want it. They are certain that the things they want are true desires from their own hearts and not the

**17**

*Distinction 9*

desires of other people. Clarity and certainty help winners pay the prices that whiners are unwilling to pay. Whiners usually want the wrong things for the wrong reasons and that's why they don't get them. Because they have allowed others to control their thoughts, they don't really know what they want.

Now, here is a key insight about the prices you must pay to get what you want. The payments don't give you what you want, they only give you the opportunity to get it. So whatever you want, you first need to pay the prices and then go get it. This lesson reminds me of the movie *The Pursuit of Happiness*, which is based on the life of Chris Gardener. In my favorite scene, the character Chris, played by actor Will Smith, is playing basketball with his young son, and his son says he wants to be a pro basketball player. At first, Chris tells his son that he can't become a pro basketball player because. . . . He then realizes his mistake and corrects himself by saying: No, that's not right, you can do whatever you want in this world. Don't ever let someone tell you what you can't do. If you want something, go get it, period.

What have you been told you can't do? I am here to tell you that you can accomplish whatever goal you aspire to. You can be, do, and have whatever you want if you are willing to pay the prices and then go get it. The purpose of this book is to inspire you to believe and encourage you to take action. I hope you will. It's not a matter of if you can, it's only a matter of if you will.

**Winners can have what they want.**

**Whiners want what they cannot have.**

# Distinction 8

Winners find a way.
Whiners find an excuse.

I once received an e-mail that posed this question: Which is more important, the power of belief or the power of persistence?

My immediate response was that belief was more important than persistence. In fact, it is belief that creates persistence. It can be challenging to persevere, especially when we're faced with failure, rejection, or loss, but belief gives us the confidence we need to persist.

Henry Ford once said, "If you think you can or you think you can't, you're right." It's a deeper truth than most people realize. Whiners continue to find excuses for two reasons. First, because things get tough, and second, because they don't believe they can prevail.

It takes a winner to "keep on keeping on" when something goes wrong. A winner sees a setback as a message to learn something new. He resolves to find a way because he believes there is a way. Whiners find an excuse because they don't believe they can succeed.

Consider a fly trapped in a room. The fly desperately bangs against the window trying to get free. His struggle is vigorous but futile, and he eventually dies. Why? It seems that the fly has only one strategy: Try harder. Had the fly simply looked around, he would have noticed that just across the room was an open door—after a few seconds of flying, he could have been free.

Many whiners behave like the fly. They try harder and harder with the wrong strategy. They find either an excuse to keep doing what they're doing or they find an excuse to quit, and in both cases, their behavior is a reflection of their limiting beliefs.

Whiners look at what they are doing and develop beliefs about whether their actions are right or wrong. Winners look at their results and, if their results are not what they want, they find different ways of being and doing, until they get the results they do want. Winners don't judge their actions as right or wrong. They focus on the results and keep adjusting their actions until they create what they want. Whiners either stay on an unsuccessful course or set a new course each time a small challenge arises.

You can find a way to get whatever it is you want, but I challenge you to first discover the kind of person you want to be. Focusing first on who you want to be empowers you to find a way to create what you want to do and have.

I wanted to be a best-selling author and empower people with simple truths that transform their lives. Although I did write a book, I went through several years of struggle and some disappointments. But because I had decided who I wanted to be first and believed I could, I found a way. I persevered, and I did.

So, who do you want to be? Winners answer that question before they decide what they want to do or have. Winners focus on being powerful and peaceful. They feed their faith and starve their fears. They understand that what they do and have is a reflection of who they are. Whiners find an excuse because they don't have a vision for who they want to be. Your vision for yourself and your life must be something you can believe in with all your heart—a vision that fills you with passion and keeps you on course.

Because whiners lack that vision, most of what they do is short-term and devoid of power and commitment. Vision empowers you to find a way, no matter what. A lack of vision causes you to find an excuse.

Whiners find an excuse because more often than not they are fulfilling someone else's vision, and the dreams of others can inspire for only a limited time. It's not wrong or bad to help someone else with their vision, but in order to have long-term passion and inspiration you must personalize it and make it your vision, too. You can make someone else's vision yours and become a winner, and in my experience, a time will come when you do get your own vision. And, just as you have served someone else's vision for a time, you will find people to help serve your vision when it is time to pursue it. Winners help other winners.

Winners can't help whiners who are unwilling to help themselves. Whiners must first help themselves by deciding: "I am going to be a winner." After making a decision with your head and a commitment with your heart to become a winner, you will find a way.

Whiners say: "I can't see it, so I don't believe it." Winners say: "I believe it—that's why I can see it." Winners have vision. "The only thing worse than being blind is having sight but no vision," is a profound and powerful quote from Helen Keller. Winners find a way because we believe there is a way and our belief helps us to see it. Vision is internal. It is seeing through eyes of faith. It is looking within your heart and seeing what is there. Winners use the power of their hearts and their heads. We consciously choose to focus our thoughts on the vision that is in our hearts.

In my experience, a vision usually shows us a destination. Visions rarely show you all the detailed steps of the journey. In order to find a way you need to find *the* way that is right for you. Let's say you have a vision to become a millionaire. Well, there are a million ways to make a million dollars. Winners find the way that is right for them to reach their goals. The way of a winner is full of lessons to be learned. Whiners find an excuse because they don't learn the lessons of the journey. Some of the lessons come from teachers called failure, rejection, and loss. Winners take the lessons they learn on their journey and keep moving forward even though the lessons might be difficult. If you are going to find a way, you must endure some hard times and be willing to get up and get going again. As long as you keep learning and moving, you will find the way that is right for you to achieve the vision that is in your heart.

Jim Rohn used to tell a story of the best definition he ever heard for the word *resolve*. He was teaching some kids about becoming successful and asked them if they knew what resolve meant. Many different answers were given that were close, but there was a little girl who hit the nail on the head. She said, "Resolve is a promise to yourself that you will never give up." Jim said that was the best he ever heard; I concur. Resolve is determination; it is the power to persevere. Strengthen your resolve by taking responsibility, paying the prices, and promising yourself that you will never give up.

**Winners find a way.**
**Whiners find an excuse.**

# Distinction 7

Winners brighten a room by entering.
Whiners brighten a room by leaving.

Winners energize people. The excitement about who they are becoming and what they are doing in life makes their enthusiasm a tangible force—it feels good just to be in their presence. Whiners, on the other hand, can be emotional vampires, draining the energy from everyone around them.

Have you ever noticed that winners attract other winners, while whiners cluster with whiners? Birds of a feather do, indeed, flock together. If you've made the decision to change from whiner to winner, it's essential to surround yourself with winners as much as possible. A warning, though: Winners will not spend

**31**

much time with those who continue to complain. To find and keep the company of winners, you will need to eliminate whining from your life.

If God had made 11 commandments, the eleventh might have been *Thou Shalt Not Whine*. I have a plaque in my home bearing that inscription, and it acts as a constant reminder that although we are all human, and we live in a world that can be more pessimistic than optimistic, we must be vigilant in choosing the words we speak.

Whiners brighten a room by leaving because they take their complaining with them. Have you noticed that whiners will actually get into a competition to see whose life is worse? No wonder winners refuse to spend time with whiners.

It's my opinion that the overwhelming majority of people fit the description of a whiner. Even my 96-year-old great-grandmother thinks so. While I was at my parents' house dropping off a copy of the Random House version of my book, *The Top 10 Distinctions between Millionaires and the Middle Class*, my great-grandmother walked by the table and picked up the book. She read the title aloud and then asked me, "Does this tell you how to be a millionaire? How do you do it?" I rattled off a few simple things, like having faith, taking risks, and refusing to complain.

She paused, and then said, "Well, there ain't gonna be many people get there."

My grandmother is right. Most people are addicted to whining, and it takes conscious effort and daily discipline to stop complaining and to become a winner.

Like becoming a millionaire, becoming a winner is a choice. Part of that choice is to stop complaining and start appreciating. Winners brighten a room by showing appreciation for life. They talk about the good things that have happened, are happening, and will happen.

In my Wisdom Creates Freedom workshop I give everyone a life-changing challenge—if you're willing to receive it, I'd like to offer it to you. The challenge is this: For ten days, do not complain. If you go one day and then complain on the second day, you must start over at day one. If you go three days without complaining, and complain on the fourth, you must again go back to day one and start over. When you can go ten days without complaining, you will have become very aware of the power of your words. You will also start to notice the winners and whiners in your life on a deeper level. Whiners are unconscious of how much they whine. Winners are aware of the power of their words, and through those words they brighten a room.

In addition to complaining, whiners are also masters of self-pity. Winners do not attend pity parties. They don't throw them for themselves and they don't respond to an invitation to attend someone else's. Self-pity is part of the darkness that leaves a room when a whiner walks out.

It's impossible to become a winner if you are wallowing in self-pity. Wallowing in self-pity is like a dog eating its own vomit or a pig rolling around in its own waste. It's no wonder winners don't spend much time with whiners. Would you want to spend a lot of time with someone who smells like vomit or crap? The reason that whiners can hang out with whiners is because they all smell the same and they are used to the stench.

Winners do, however, spend some time with whiners trying to help them clean themselves off. I love the fact that Jesus took time to be with whiners and influence them for the good. Winners work with whiners until they can tell that the whiner is not willing to grow. If a whiner is committed to staying the same—well, let's just say that there is only so much of the smell that a winner can take.

You might say that winners make a room smell better by entering and whiners make a room smell better by leaving. How do you smell? What do winners pick up on when they are around you? Are you aware of your light and your darkness? We all have the potential to brighten a room or darken it. Winners focus on walking in light. They are appreciative and focus more on the good in this world than the bad. They brighten a room by encouraging others, congratulating others, and refusing to speak poorly of others. Whiners discourage others, compete with each other on how bad their lives are, and gossip.

Becoming a winner demands that you focus on the positive. Winning is a choice. Choose to appreciate, encourage, and find the good in yourself and others. Choose to be a winner and help light the way for those that follow.

When you become a person who can brighten a room you will have become a true leader. True leaders shine light on the paths of others and help them see who they can become and where they can go. All winners are leaders. We do not lead by force or manipulation; we lead by power and persuasion. Leading by power is simply doing what we can to achieve our goals. Power is the ability to act. Leading by force is to impose your will on another. Persuading people is to help them see that they want to come with you. Manipulating people is to try and make people feel like they have to go with you. Power and persuasion are the light that helps people to see who they can be. Force and manipulation are the darkness that causes people to be confused.

When a winner uses their strengths to do what they want to do and others see it, it empowers others to believe they can too. Identifying your strengths and using them increases your light and helps you see who you are and who you can still become.

Winners know their strengths and their weaknesses. We consistently use our strengths to become more successful. We do not waste our time trying to do things that require strengths that we don't have. We humbly acknowledge that there are many things we are not good at. Instead of feeling bad about our weaknesses, we are thankful for our strengths and choose to use them every day. Feeling bad is part of the darkness that others feel when they are around someone who is focused on their weaknesses. The gratitude that winners have for their strengths and the success they achieve by using them is the light that other people see.

Most people respect success because when they see someone else who succeeds it encourages them to believe they can become successful too. There is a small number of people who resent successful people because they have been lied to about who they can become and what they can do. The darkness of lies blinds people to the truth of who they are. The truth is you have strengths and if you use them consistently you will become a winner and achieve success. Winners brighten a room by believing and walking in the truth of who they are. By using their strengths, they become successful and encourage others to do the same. All the winners I know have a common belief and that is: If I can do it, so can you.

**Winners brighten a room by entering.**
**Whiners brighten a room by leaving.**

# Distinction 6

Winners listen twice as much as they talk.
Whiners talk twice as much as they listen.

You may be surprised to discover that the greatest communication skill you can master has nothing to do with talking. The greatest communication skill you can master is listening.

By learning to be a committed listener you can develop deeper and more meaningful relationships. When you focus your attention on listening to understand rather than listening to respond, you learn more, connect better, and the conversation reaches a deeper level.

The tendency in our society is to interrupt people while they are talking. Someone says something that

**41**

triggers a thought in our minds, and we feel a need to blurt that thought out. As soon as we think we know what they are saying, we interrupt to share our opinions or beliefs about the topic. Sadly, though, when we interrupt people like this, we usually miss what they are really trying to say.

Winners learn to listen and they continually work to master the skill. Whiners can't keep their mouths shut. They ramble on and on, oblivious to how many times they interrupt others. Pay attention during your next conversation. How often do you feel a need to cut short the speech of others? Do you interrupt people more than you sincerely listen to them?

If you reflect for a moment, you will find that when you speak with someone that you really admire— someone you truly respect—you tend to listen more than you talk. The lesson here is not that you shouldn't interrupt people you respect—after all, winners respect all people equally—but that when you interrupt, you communicate a lack of respect to the person you are speaking to.

Another critical distinction is that winners listen with their hearts, while whiners listen only with their heads. Our cognitive processes—our "heads"—are

*The Top 10 Distinctions between Winners and Whiners*

reactive and dominated by our ego. That ego is proud of what we think we know, and wants to prove it. When we use our emotional intelligence—our "hearts"—to listen, we connect with others on a more profound level. We try to truly understand what they are feeling and saying, not what we think they are saying. Winning relationships are formed by those who practice listening with their hearts; the inability to grasp this distinction is at the root of countless failed marriages and business partnerships.

When you become a committed listener, you are becoming a winner. Here's another challenge for you. For the next 10 days, commit to being a listener in every conversation you have. Resist the urge to interrupt, or even speak. Just listen with your heart. You'll find that this challenge will also help with the challenge of not complaining—after all, if you're talking less, you'll probably be complaining less. So, for 10 days, don't complain and practice being a committed listener. These two simple challenges will put you on the path of a winner.

Have you ever wondered why God gave us two ears and one mouth? I think that it's a clear message that we should listen twice as much as we talk.

Many people are addicted to talking and do quite the opposite—they talk at least twice as much as they listen. What causes this imbalance?

Once again, we find ego at the root of the problem. Many people try desperately to prove their points at any cost, and persuade others to see their opinions as right. Some people can't stand it when others disagree with them. And, although it is nice when people agree with us, winners understand that people have their own opinions, and trying to talk someone into a new point of view isn't the wisest use of time.

It's funny to me that if you let a whiner talk and talk and talk, you can watch them confuse themselves and then try to make sense out of what they just said.

Whiners are good at justifying their beliefs and finding reasons why they are right and we are wrong. Whiners don't have deep relationships because their communication is so shallow. Even in conversation with others, whiners are usually having a monologue, not a dialogue. Whiners are so stuck in their own perceptions that it's extremely difficult for them to consider what someone else is saying, especially if it differs from their opinions.

This distinction reveals a simple, yet very profound, secret to success: Talk less and listen more. If you do this, then you will start learning more and seeing the world differently, which leads to new experiences and ideas.

Talking less and listening more is a great way to increase your inner peace. Peace is a powerful state, one that leads to prosperity. If you want to increase your peace and decrease your stress, talk less.

Listening more attentively to others will also empower you to listen more to your own heart. That small still voice that we call "gut feeling" or "intuition" becomes clearer and easier to hear when you are quiet. Talk less and listen more—you may even be surprised to hear your heavenly Father communicate with you. When you are in a conversation, say only what you really need to say and then simply listen.

It is harder for some people to listen than others. If this statement hits home for you, then I have the following advice from my own life. If that is not you, and you tend to be able to listen rather well, then this section will help you have a better understanding of someone that you might think is a jerk but really isn't.

As I wrote in Distinction 7, we all have strengths and weaknesses, and sometimes our greatest strengths can at times be a weakness. For example, some people are good at research and gathering ample information before they make a decision. However, if a person gets bogged down in too many details, they can suffer from the paralysis of analysis and miss an opportunity because they took too long to make a decision. Other people have the ability to process things very quickly and make decisions quickly.

Some people say they are a "type A" personality. These people, of whom I am one, can make decisions more quickly because we have a strong sense of confidence and direction in our lives. Our strength of confidence can at times become the weakness of arrogance. This means we think we already know what is best in a situation, so instead of listening to understand, we may interrupt someone because we think we already know. This has led to some unnecessary problems in my own life. There are some mistakes I have made that I could have avoided if I had listened more carefully to what others were trying to tell me. If you have a type A personality, then

*The Top 10 Distinctions between Winners and Whiners*

you probably understand exactly what I am saying. If you are not a type A, but you know someone who is, you probably have a certain level of respect for them, but there are times when they can be almost unbearable!

When you have to engage in conversation with someone who has a hard time listening, you need to begin the conversation with one or all of the following statements.

Please hear me out completely before you respond.

I have something important to share with you; please listen carefully.

This is going to take a minute, so please be patient as I explain this.

Of course, we should hear people out, listen carefully, and be patient before we respond. That's the point of this Distinction, but sometimes we don't do those things. It's important to remember that everyone thinks they are right from their point of view, so when someone interrupts you to share their point of view, don't take it personally, just listen. Whether you are the type A personality or the detailed person or somewhere in between, if you will take responsibility to be a committed listener you will create deeper and more fulfilling relationships, which is a big part of being a winner.

**Winners listen twice as much as they talk.**
**Whiners talk twice as much as they listen.**

# Distinction 5

Winners enjoy life's journeys.
Whiners put their joy in the destinations.

L ife is a series of journeys and destinations. Winners enjoy them both, but if you learn to find joy in the journey, you will experience a lot more of it. The joy of reaching a destination lasts only for a brief moment.

People tend to focus on where they're going. When they get there, though, they feel good for about a minute and then start looking for another destination. Learn to enjoy where you are. Yes, keep climbing, but don't make all of your joy dependent on achievement—make a decision to be happy here and now. Don't put your happiness off until a point in the

**51**

future, for that is a great deception. If you think you will be happy tomorrow, remember that tomorrow never arrives.

Winners live in the present. They have goals and plans for the future, but they have learned to take action now with joy. Joy is strength for the journey. It empowers us to keep going, even when we are tempted to quit. Whiners quit easily because they don't allow the power of joy to flow until they achieve or arrive.

Since whiners put their joy off until they achieve something or arrive somewhere, they walk through life in a weakened condition. The weakness causes a lack of perseverance. Whiners tire and give up because they just don't have the energy. Joy is energy to finish the journeys of life, and joy is a choice.

There are many journeys in life and we often find ourselves on more than one at the same time. School is a journey. Marriage is a journey. Parenting is a journey. Your career is a journey. Going on vacation can be a journey. Losing a loved one is a journey. Financial freedom is a journey. There are hundreds of journeys we can take in our lifetime. The key to finishing them is to make each journey with joy.

Fortunately, enjoying the journeys as well as the fleeting moments of the destinations is something we can all choose to learn. Here are three keys to help you experience the joys of the journey: growing, gratitude, and focus.

## Growing

I believe growing is one of the main purposes of life. We are not happy if we are not becoming the best we can be. If you're in school, for example, then you should be growing in specialized knowledge. If you're in a marriage, then you should be growing in love and understanding. We grow in different areas at different times in our lives.

Life demands growth, and each time we try to stay the same, we experience pain, not joy. If you are on a parenting journey, then you should be growing as an example of wisdom, and becoming aware that your attitude and actions are affecting the journeys of your children.

In truth, our attitude and actions probably affect more people's journeys than we realize. If you are taking a short journey called a vacation, you can be learning how quickly life goes and how quickly the joys of destinations are gone. If you are taking the journey called losing a loved one, you can grow in understanding how precious life is and learn to build deeper relationships with those who are still with you.

Winners grow and experience joy. Whiners try to stay the same and experience pain.

## Gratitude

Think of something or someone that you are thankful for right now. Seriously, do it right now—and then notice how you feel. Gratitude affects our mood. Gratitude generates joy. If you want to increase your joy for the journeys of your life, then increase your gratitude. Winners cultivate gratitude in their lives as one of the fastest and greatest ways to experience joy.

## Focus

What you focus on is what you feel. Focus on the good in your journey and you'll feel good. Focus on the bad and you'll feel bad. This power of focus is the power to control your feelings.

Your mind can hold only one thought at a time, so make it a good one. Every journey contains some good you can focus on. Even during the loss of a loved one we can focus on appreciating our family and friends. We can focus on the good memories we have. We always have a choice of where we direct our focus. And where we direct it determines whether we experience joy or pain.

So, as you experience your journey, keep growing, cultivating gratitude, and focusing on the good. Make joy your responsibility; do not be dependent on other people or destinations. Winners create joy right where they are. The present moment is all that exists—learn to live in it. Focusing too much on the past or future steals your joy. Whiners live their lives regretting the past and fearing the future more than they live in the present.

The rare moments of joy that whiners experience occur because they briefly become aware of the present moment. Winners continually practice being present because they know that is where their strength and joy flow from. Being present allows you to enjoy the journeys and the destinations of life. Being absent creates suffering and pain. When you focus too much on the destination, you miss the beautiful moments of your life. Learn to enjoy the journey. Grow, be thankful, and focus on the good.

Winners believe the truth that life is good. Find the good in your life and you will find the joy in your life. Life is good is not just a t-shirt or bumper sticker. It is a fundamental truth. Now notice I did not say that life is easy. Life is not easy, but it is good. Many of the journeys we take in life are downright hard, but in the midst of the hard times we can find the good if we look for it. Hard times happen to us all.

Whiners whine about life being hard, and make up excuses for their lives because of it. Winners accept the fact that life is hard and choose to grow. Winners express gratitude for the hard times because of the lessons we learned during them. The lessons of life make us stronger, and as we get stronger life does become easier. The journeys and lessons of life are like exercises – they make us healthier and stronger. Have you ever worked out in a gym and been sore the next day? The reason for the soreness is that you were doing something that was hard. If you continue to go back to the gym, the soreness will lessen and the weight that was once hard becomes relatively easy.

Although life was once hard for winners it becomes relatively easy, after a while, because we keep learning and growing, we keep cultivating gratitude, and we keep finding the good and focusing on it.

So life is good and life is hard at the same time. Winners know this, accept it, and work with it. Whiners make their lives harder than they have to be because they resist the lessons instead of growing; they complain instead of being grateful, and they look for the bad and find it, focus on it, and feel it. Life is hard but the hard times are good because they give us the opportunity to become stronger, better. and wiser. Just as whiners can make their lives worse, winners know we can make our lives better. Life is good and you can make it even better if you choose to be a winner.

**Winners enjoy life's journeys.**
**Whiners put their joy in the destinations.**

# Distinction 4

Winners build friendships.
Whiners destroy friendships.

Friendships are one of the most valuable and precious things that we can possess in this life. What does it mean to be a friend? It means to look out for the best interests of another human being. Of course, problems in friendships occur when friends have different opinions of what those best interests are.

True friends will do whatever they can to work through their differences. Have you ever had a friend become angry with you because you didn't agree with him? Have you ever gotten angry at a friend because of a misunderstanding? People have different perceptions and opinions and, as a result, we have misunderstandings.

Winners understand this and choose to work through their differences instead of becoming angry about them. A classic example is when a husband and wife are talking and the husband is not hearing what his wife is really saying, or vice versa. Later, one will say to the other, "I asked you to do this," and the other will say, "No, you didn't." Within moments, the situation deteriorates into anger.

We do not always hear what other people are trying to communicate to us. True friends respect each other and listen with their hearts.

Winners are able to build deep and meaningful friendships because they acknowledge that their friends have perceptions and opinions.

A perception is the way you see or understand something. An opinion is a belief you have, based on your past results. If you want to build more friendships, then acknowledge that perceptions and opinions are not absolute truths. Just because we see things differently from someone else doesn't mean that we are right, even if our ego demands it.

Winners don't immediately assume they are right. Winners practice looking at situations from different perspectives. Whiners, on the other hand, almost always assume that their way is the only way.

Ego has destroyed millions of friendships. It is impossible to build long-lasting friendships without humility. Humility is the ability to learn and grow. Humility is the willingness to let someone be as they are and accept them that way. It is the power to love people unconditionally. Humility is a willingness to forgive. All long-lasting friendships are built on humility and forgiveness. And, while we will always have misunderstandings in our friendships, winners know this and choose to build stronger friendships when they occur. Humility is the secret to friendships, and it is the key to becoming a winner.

We've all had moments when we thought we were right, but later, upon reflection or more information, we acknowledged we were wrong. Our perceptions and opinions are limited. The more you hold onto your way of seeing and believing, the more difficult it will be to build friendships.

When we try to demand that someone else change his perception and see things as we do, we have stopped being a friend and started to become arrogant. Arrogance is an unwillingness to even consider another perspective, and whiners destroy friendships because of it. Ego is rooted in arrogance, and when whiners allow their egos to run their lives, it ruins their lives, too.

Winners know when to be dependent, independent, and interdependent. There are times when things are beyond our control and we must depend on others, and there are times when our friends need to lean on us. Then, there are times when we need to stand on our own two feet. Wisdom is knowing exactly when to be dependent, independent, and interdependent.

There are also times when we need others and they need us. Learning when to be interdependent is a key to being a winner. Interdependency is what friendship is all about. It is where miracles can occur. Being interdependent allows the wisdom and knowledge of both people to flow freely, allowing great things to happen.

Whiners don't know much about being interdependent. They are usually dependent victims or independently arrogant. Being interdependent is where love, humility, and forgiveness flow. It is an understanding that I have something to contribute and so do you. It is balance between needing each other and wanting each other. Interdependence focuses on what is best for everyone. Whiners want things on their terms. Winners want what is best for all. Winners are other-people minded and inclusive. Whiners are selfish and exclusive.

Look closely at the word friendship. It is made of two words, friend and ship. When two or more people board the same ship, their path is one of unity and peace. When two or more people want to go in different directions, there is only division and stress. A key to building friendships is to find the things you agree on. Accept the fact that there are things that you are not going to agree on, but focus on what you do agree on. That focus leads to smooth sailing away from the storms of disagreement that destroy friendships.

Deep and meaningful relationships don't just happen; they must be built. Building anything takes time, especially building friendships. When you focus on building friendships you are creating unity. There is strength in unity. United we stand, divided we fall, is just as true for two friends as it is for an entire nation. The essence of building friendships is to stay focused on what we agree on. No two people agree on everything all of the time, but the more we work at staying focused on what we do agree on, the stronger our friendships will become. When the inevitable small disagreements arise, we choose to overlook them and remain true to each other. When the more serious disagreements arise, the ones that are just too big to overcome, we should do our best to part our ways in peace. It is painful and unfortunate when friends become enemies. For the most part this is usually the result of lacking communication, trust, or humility. When there is too much assuming, accusing, arguing, and arrogance between two people, it is impossible to build a friendship between them. Winners understand that there are many situations that just aren't worth making into an issue. Winners are good at letting things go. The long-term mutual benefits of friendship are much better than the selfish short-term gains of winning an argument. Whiners destroy friendships by arguing over small issues. Winners overlook the small disagreements and rarely argue even over the big ones. Always remember that you can stand for

*The Top 10 Distinctions between Winners and Whiners*

what you believe in and make your point known without arguing.

The reason winners build friendships is because we understand the value of friendship. True friends are valuable; they are more valuable than money. Winners understand that as they build friendships they become truly wealthy. Winners also understand that whoever they build friendships with can help them build financial wealth (but that's another subject!). Building friendships is important and, who you build them with is important also. The truth is your friends are affecting your life for either the positive or the negative. Choose your friends wisely. Let's finish this Distinction by giving you three questions to consider.

**1.** Who am I consciously choosing to build friend-ships with?
**2.** How are my friendships affecting my life?
**3.** Do I need to focus on building some new friendships?

**Winners build friendships.**
**Whiners destroy them.**

# Distinction 3

Winners think big.
Whiners think small.

M ost of us have been trained from the time we were very young to think small—we've been taught only to survive, and survival thinking is narrow in its focus. When you shift your focus beyond survival, to the larger goal of freedom, you will find your thinking will expand, too.

Thinking big requires a conscious choice, and once we begin to make this choice on a consistent basis, we begin to understand how limiting our perceptions have been. When we choose to think bigger, we start to see possibilities, and our perceptions and opinions begin to transform.

Faith is the belief in good things happening, and thinking big is the fruit of that faith. By exercising your faith, you experience positive feelings and emotions. Thinking big produces excitement and joy. Thinking small produces fear and anxiety. Fear is to believe that bad things are going to happen. Small thinking is the fruit of fear. Winners exercise their faith by taking action towards their deep desires. Whiners live in fear and ignore their dreams and goals.

I believe everyone has a big dream. Winners pursue theirs with belief that it can be achieved. Since whiners think small, they doubt that their big dream is possible. Their lack of faith can be seen in the difference between the questions that winners and whiners ask themselves. For example, winners ask, "How can I?" while whiners ask, "Can I?"

Winners assume they can—they just need to learn how. Whiners want to believe they can, but their small thinking and doubts prevent it. They ask, "Can I?" because there is an underlying fear that they cannot. It's always a mistake to assume the negative—if you're going to make assumptions, make them positive ones. Ask yourself, "How can I achieve my big dream?"

Believe that your big dream is possible. Have faith in it. By focusing on your big dream with faith, you will start thinking bigger.

Faith, like fear, is a choice, and most of us were taught to choose fear at a very young age. Winners have a time in their lives when they are confronted with their fears and they choose to have faith and pursue their purposes with passion. When whiners are confronted with their fears they choose to retreat back to a life of small living.

If you struggle with fear, doubts, and small thinking, understand that these are only perceptions, and that perceptions can be changed. Just because you hold a belief now, doesn't mean you have to hold that belief forever. We can change our beliefs. We can alter our opinions. Winners are not afraid to question what they believe and see if their belief is limiting them. Winners understand that beliefs influence our behaviors and our behaviors influence our results. They look at their results and if they are not what they want, they go to work on their beliefs.

Whiners assume their beliefs are right and blame their results on someone or something else. Remember, your results are your responsibility. If they are not what you want, then work on expanding your beliefs. Think bigger. Expand your perception of what is possible. The reason that whiners continue to think small is because they keep the same beliefs.

Thinking big will require you to change your beliefs. Winners work on their thoughts. Thinking is the process of asking yourself questions. Winners learn to ask themselves bigger questions, which, of course, deliver bigger answers. By asking new and bigger questions, we come up with new ideas of what is possible. Big questions expand our minds to the point that we find things we used to think were impossible are now within our grasp. Whiners are rigid in their beliefs. They refuse to consider things that are different from what they already believe, and so they remain whiners. The only way for a whiner to become a winner is to think bigger.

Thinking bigger requires new beliefs of what is possible. Thinking big requires faith, bigger questions, and new beliefs. Choose to have that faith, to ask yourself those bigger questions, and to work on expanding your beliefs.

A friend once posted a comment on my Facebook page that said, "The secrets of success will only work

*The Top 10 Distinctions between Winners and Whiners*

if you do." To add to that thought, one of my favorite sayings is, "Faith without work is dead." Thinking big requires work. Einstein once said that thinking is hard work; that's why so few people do it. Thinking big will take you outside of your comfort zone. It's not easy when you first stretch beyond your comfort zone, but if you work at thinking big then your comfort zone will get bigger. When it does, then you can be more, do more, and have more. When you expand your mind you expand your comfort zone. You expand your mind by embracing challenges. Be willing to work on your life in every area of your life. Look at the big picture. Don't just think about where you are, also think about where you are going. Don't just think about who you are, also think about who you are becoming. Thinking big will change you. Thinking big will take you to new places.

Thinking big has benefits; thinking small has consequences. Some of the benefits of thinking big are peace and joy. Some of the consequences of thinking small are stress and unhappiness. Winners are happy because we think big. Whiners are unhappy because they think small. Another benefit that goes beyond happiness is enthusiasm. It is exciting to think about

**75**

the possibilities of life. Practice thinking about what's possible for you and you will find yourself living with enthusiasm and that will energize you. The energy of enthusiasm is powerful and contagious. The enthusiasm you generate by thinking big will influence those around you to think bigger and become winners too.

**Winners think big.**

**Whiners think small.**

# Distinction 2

Winners are focus-minded.
Whiners are scatterbrained.

Have you ever felt overwhelmed, or experienced the anxiety of having too much coming at you at once? We all have, at one time or another, and during those moments the stress of being overwhelmed reduces our ability to think, create, and make decisions.

There are two significant causes for feeling overwhelmed. The first is complaining. When you complain, you play the victim, talk excessively, destroy friendships, and think small. Whining overwhelms people and destroys peace of mind.

Remember that winners don't whine and whiners don't win. Winners live with peace of mind. Whiners live in a near-constant state of feeling overwhelmed.

The second source of feeling overwhelmed is being scatterbrained. As long as you are scatterbrained, you will be stressed. When you learn to focus on your top priorities, your mind becomes quiet and you find yourself at peace. A focused mind is powerful and can create new ideas to solve problems.

Ideas can flow from a focused mind. A scattered brain is weak and starts to shut down. For a scattered brain, creativity is next to impossible.

Our minds can handle only a limited number of things. While some people may be able to juggle ten or more things at a time, others may only be able to deal with two or three. When we try to focus on more than we are capable of, we feel overwhelmed.

The solution is to simplify your life.

Winners simplify their lives by breaking them down into categories. Whiners complicate their lives by thinking in terms of all and everything. What are your priorities in each area of life? What are your spiritual priorities? What are your emotional priorities?

What are your mental priorities? What are your physical priorities? What are your financial priorities?

Start with your responsibilities. What are you responsible for? It is my experience that we often take responsibility for things that we shouldn't and neglect the things we should. The feeling of being overwhelmed is deceptive because it comes even when we are trying to do a lot of good things. We can't do everything. We can't even do everything that we want to do, but we can do everything that we need to do. We get so scatterbrained by trying to do too much. Sometimes our desires create enormous amounts of stress for us because we think we have to fulfill them. We don't.

Sometimes you bounce your focus around from things that you regret in the past, to fears you have about the future, to the things demanding your attention right now. When you are overwhelmed, you are living in reaction. To become a winner, you need to move from reaction to creation.

In those moments of feeling overwhelmed, it is critical to reprioritize your life by asking yourself: "What is really important right now?" You have to find out how many things you can juggle and still maintain your peace. After you know that, then focus your mind on the most important things. If you can handle seven things at a time without feeling overwhelmed, then find the top seven things you need to focus on and let go of the rest. Focus on what's most important right now.

You can either use your mind by focusing it—or be used by it by being scatterbrained.

There are some things you think you want, but once you get them you realize that they weren't what you wanted after all. Desires have the potential to drive people crazy, and it's critical to learn to discern between what you really want and need versus what you think would make you happy.

If you focus your mind on what's really important, you'll find that you can live quite well with less. The push for more and more in our society is destroying millions of lives. Learn to simplify and find the few things that truly bring you peace. Peace is not found in the hurry and worry of our society. It's found by focusing your mind on what is most important to you.

By focusing your mind, you create peace of mind. By being scatterbrained you create stress. Winners know that stress is all too often self-inflicted and we know that peace is produced by focusing on our priorities. There are many good things that could be demanding your attention but it is your responsibility to determine where to direct your energies. It is true that good is often the enemy of the great. Winners want the great, so we practice focusing our minds. Whiners get easily distracted from their priorities and that causes them to settle for less than their best. Focusing your mind empowers you to move from good to great.

How do you focus your mind? The answer is, by asking empowering questions. Questions control your focus. To harness the power of focus you must learn to ask yourself empowering questions. I wrote in detail about this in Distinction 1 of *The Top 10 Distinctions between Millionaires and the Middle Class*. I also gave nine empowering questions in that book that help clarify your vision for life. Now, I want to give you a few more empowering questions that I personally use very often, almost daily. I believe they will help you get and stay focused.

Learn to consistently ask yourself: What are my highest priorities? What is the best use of my time right now? In your financial life, ask yourself: What are my highest income producing activities? In your family life, ask yourself: How can I invest more meaningful time with my family?

This is a simple but profound strategy to get and stay focused. The questions you ask yourself determine what you are focusing on and what you focus on determines how you feel. You can control your feelings by the questions you ask yourself. Get good at creating good feelings in your life and you will take more good actions that will create more good results in your life. Focus determines feelings, feelings affect our actions, and our actions create our results. It is truly amazing what you can create in your life when you focus your mind.

**Winners are focus-minded.**
**Whiners are scatterbrained**.

# Distinction 1

Winners create positive meanings.
Whiners create negative meanings.

How do you define the seasons, events, and moments of your life? How do you view the circumstances and people around you? Winners have learned to look for and find the good in their lives and the world. Whiners seek—and eventually find—the negative aspects of their lives.

One of the most powerful things you can learn to do is create positive meanings. Even for seemingly negative events, there exists a silver lining. Seek it, and you shall find it. What are you seeking? The good or the bad?

You get what you look for in life. It's worth repeating: You get what you look for in life. Most people take the seasons, events, and moments of their lives and define them as negative. Even when life offers them a wonderful opportunity, they miss it. Why? Because they simply aren't looking for it.

Winners find the opportunity in every difficulty because they seek it. Whiners find the difficulty in every opportunity because they, too, find what they seek.

What is your initial mental reaction when faced with a difficult experience? Do you look for the good or the bad? Almost every event in our lives can be viewed as negative or positive. Why not choose the empowering path?

Whiners view the world through a negative lens, a damaging perspective that creates needless suffering. And, although suffering can bring its own positive lessons into our lives, whiners experience needless mountains of self-inflicted struggle and pain. The meanings you create in your life determine whether you experience joy or pain. They have the power to get you through the tough times and they also have the power to keep you stuck for a long time. How do you define your experiences?

One of the most destructive things I see whiners do is stack several events of their lives and create negative meanings for each one. Another way to ruin your life is to define entire seasons of your life as negative. Many people do this in business and marriage. They look back on a season, remember a few negative moments, and label the entire season as negative.

Winners remember the good times from their past. They even think back to some of the tough times with gratitude—because they learned so much going through them. Most seasons have both positive and negative experiences in them—choose to remember the positive moments. In your present moments, learn to call them good. If you're going through a tough time right now, is it possible that it contains a hidden blessing? Yes, it's very possible. Strive to create positive meanings in your present circumstances. As you do this more and more, you will think back on these moments with joy and gratitude.

In my book *The Top 10 Distinctions between Millionaires and the Middle Class*, the number one distinction is that millionaires ask themselves empowering questions while the middle class ask themselves disempowering questions. People will remain whiners as long as they ask disempowering questions and create negative meanings. When you learn to ask yourself empowering questions and create positive meanings, then you will become a winner.

There is one specific question that we always (yes, always) ask ourselves during an experience. The question is: What does this mean? Most people are unaware of the questions and answers that are continually going through their minds, but winners are conscious of this inner dialogue. They create empowering questions and positive answers. Learn to duplicate that, and your life will be transformed. You will move from fear to faith, from stress to peace, from darkness to light. Whatever you are going through, find the good.

Winners understand that there are always many different perspectives we can choose to view an event or circumstance from. Your point of view is yours to control. You can change your perspectives if you choose. Winners work on their perspectives and that makes them powerful people, while whiners usually only look at things from one point of view, their own. Winners and whiners see things differently because winners choose their perceptions based on the results they want in their lives. People create different results because of different perceptions. Millionaires look at money from a different perspective than people who are middle class. Healthy people look at health and nutrition from a different perspective than people who are unhealthy. And winners look at life from a different perspective than whiners do. Winners practice looking at each area of life from different perspectives so we can experience as much of life as possible. Life has more to offer than any one of us can experience alone. By practicing looking at life from different perspectives you can and will experience more. It will change you. You will become a different person, a better person.

The meanings you create about situations are simply the perspectives you have about them. Changing your perspectives is to change the way you think. Changing the way you think is not easy, but you can make it fun. Winners enjoy creating positive meanings because it increases their peace of mind and raises them above their situations. Whiners are under their situations, winners are over them. You can learn to fly and look down from above, or you can be depressed and feel beneath your situations. Choosing to create positive meanings can lift you up from a pit of depression and put you on top of a mountain.

Practice looking at life from different perspectives; I guarantee you will learn to love your life. As you practice looking at life from a positive perspective, you will get good at creating positive meanings and you will be a winner. You will start winning more consistently and living life to the fullest. You can create a great life by creating positive meanings.

**Winners create positive meanings.**
**Whiners create negative meanings.**

# *What Now?*

Read this book often. Repetition is one of the primary ways we train our minds to think differently. When we think different, we act different, and achieve different results.

Share copies of this book with the appropriate people in your life so you can discuss the Distinctions and learn from each other's experiences and perspectives.

Go to keithcameronsmith.com and register for the Wise Distinctions e-mail so you can receive continued support in developing a Winner's mentality. You can also get more information about the Wisdom Creates Freedom Workshop and the Wisdom Creates Winners Workshop taught by Keith.